GW01607118

The Elephant and the Flower

What is this book? It is small and it is simple. Sometimes it is funny and most times it is happy. It is only fiction because the jungle in which the stories take place has never really been discovered.

What is it about? It is about a very small elephant (roughly two and a bit inches) and a flower that walks because it does not wish to remain rooted in the same spot all the time.

Why was it written? It was written because before it was written no Plinkinplonks, Kuputte-birds, side-stepping pigs or Forests of Moonbeams existed. And now they do.

Who was it written for? It was written for children with the hope that their parents might read it to them and with the hope that when they are able to, they will read it themselves.

What ages is it for? For those who cannot read, and for those who can read, and for those who won't read but will listen, and for a girl who is now five and who lives in Winchester and who wanted one day to go walking with a flower and asked why it could not move. And now it can—every time she picks up this book.

* * * *

The Elephant and the Flower is Brian Patten's first book for children. He was born in Liverpool in 1946 and has published two books of poetry, *Little Johnny's Confession* and *Notes to the Hurrying Man* (Allen and Unwin, 1967 and 1969).

by Brian Patten

Little Johnny's Confession

Notes to the Hurrying Man

Record
Brian Patten Reading His Poetry
(Caedmon LP, 1970)

The Elephant & the Flower

Almost-fables

by BRIAN PATTEN

Illustrated by MEG RUTHERFORD

London GEORGE ALLEN AND UNWIN LTD

FIRST PUBLISHED IN 1970

SBN 04 823092 8

PRINTED IN GREAT BRITAIN
IN 10 ON 12 PT UNIVERS
BY JARROLD AND SONS LTD
NORWICH

In a jungle that was almost a forest
And in a forest that was almost a wood
And in a wood that was almost a garden
There once lived an elephant and a
Flower and a pig and a giraffe and
A Kuputte-bird. There was also a
Hyena there and a Plinkinplonk and
Monkeys as well;
and of course
there was a
Forest of Moonbeams, and a silver
Ant that dreamt of silence, and a
River that told the strangest stories.

For Karen
who wondered about
flowers

Contents

The Flower and the Elephant

There was once a flower that lived on a hill in the jungle. When the flower was very small, the wind had blown it hundreds of miles across the jungle. It landed in a place where no other flowers like itself lived. It was the only flower that could really walk. Although it met the blossoms and the lilies, they were much older, and fixed in their ways. And so it soon became bored with them. They just wanted to talk and sit all day on the same branches and in the same ponds. When the flower said things like 'Let's go somewhere' they looked indignant and thought the flower very strange. 'Flowers don't go running round playing games,' they said.

And so the flower that could walk grew up alone.

And once there was an elephant no larger than a flower. Its mother was embarrassed by its size, and so put it on a leaf and floated it downstream. 'The jungle gods will take care of him,' she thought. The stream changed into a river and the river flowed past the hill where the flower lived.

One day the flower was standing by the side of the river having a drink. The leaf with the elephant on came floating past. 'Hello,' said the flower when the leaf was quite near. 'I never knew elephants sailed on leaves.'

'They don't usually,' said the elephant. 'Not even very tiny ones. But that's beside the point. I'm not a very good swimmer and the leaf's just about to sink. You'd better help me.'

'Certainly,' said the flower, and it pulled the leaf to the edge of the stream with a long thin twig.

The elephant scrambled off the leaf and up on to the river bank. It stood there, happy to be back on firm ground. It looked round at the green tangle of trees. 'This is a lovely place,' it said. 'Do you mind if I stay?'

'Of course not,' said the flower. 'You can stay as long as you like.'

And so they became friends. They stayed together on the hill and lived on things like apples. The elephant did not worry about being very small, and the flower just laughed when the old blossoms and lilies said it should always stay in the same place.

Why the Nightingale Left the Jungle

One summer evening the flower and the elephant sat together in the jungle and listened to the nightingale singing.

'It makes me very sleepy,' said the flower. 'When I hear its song I dream of all the colours I could be. I could be green like the grass or yellow like the sun. I could be as white as the moon, or as brown as the crocodile who lives in the marshes. Pink as the flamingo, even. I could be . . .'

'You are very poetic,' interrupted the elephant, who was not very interested in any colour but its own nice shade of browny grey.

'What do you dream about?' asked the flower.

'Only of being the very largest elephant in the world.'

A hyena was hiding in the bushes, listening to their conversation. It was a very ugly hyena, all thin and scraggy.

'I'll play a joke on them,' it thought. And from the bush it shouted, 'It's the vulture singing, not the nightingale, you idiots!' And the hyena laughed so loud it drowned the nightingale's song.

'Who's that?' asked the flower.

The hyena did not answer. Instead it laughed even louder and ruined the nightingale's song. It laughed so loud that the song was crushed against the leaves and died.

The nightingale grew very worried. 'I think the jungle's laughing at me,' it said. 'I'll fly to a place where my song will be appreciated.'

And so the nightingale flew away. It flew above the trees and mountains and was soon many miles from the jungle.

'I'll not go back there,' it thought.

When it was gone the jungle grew silent.

'Now I won't be able to dream of all the different colours I could be,' said the flower.

'Nor I of being a very large elephant,' said the elephant. And then it grew angry and shouted out into the jungle, 'You're a very stupid creature, whatever you are!'

'Hu!' grunted the hyena. 'They don't appreciate my jokes.' And it crept slyly away from the bush, not wanting the flower and the elephant to see it go.

'They just don't understand them,' it thought. All night it wandered about the jungle, waking everyone up and telling them very weak jokes, and when nobody laughed it had to laugh itself.

It bullied every little creature it could find.

'If you don't laugh at my jokes I'll eat you,' it said, and they were so frightened they could not laugh anyway. So they got eaten. And so everything stayed clear of the hyena. Even the birds, who it could not reach, stopped singing when it passed under their nests. It became the least loved creature in the jungle, but still it kept on laughing.

'I think it's laughing at its own foolishness,' said the elephant. But the flower wasn't so sure.

But whatever they said, the nightingale never returned to the jungle, and ever since that time the hyena has been wandering alone, looking for someone to appreciate its jokes.

The Talkative Butterfly

'Hello,' said the butterfly.

'Hello,' said the flower, 'you've been away a long time.'

'What do you mean, a long time?' asked the butterfly. 'I only came out of my cocoon a few hours ago.'

'You mean you are another butterfly then?' asked the flower. 'Strange, you look just like a butterfly I saw last year.'

'Impossible,' said the butterfly. 'We don't usually live a bit as long as that. The life of a butterfly is short and sweet,' it quoted. 'I'm exactly two hours old and I don't know very much about anything.'

'Well, for a start,' said the flower, 'I'm a flower and my friend's an elephant.' The flower pointed to the elephant who was sleeping under the hill. 'In fact he is the smallest elephant in the world.'

'How long has *he* been born?' asked the butterfly.

'A long time,' said the flower.

'Really? More than two days?' asked the butterfly.

'Of course,' said the flower. 'Many more days than that.'

'Does he know many things?' the butterfly wanted to know.

The flower looked at its friend, who was snoring rather loudly. 'I don't think he really knows anything,' it said. 'Why do you ask?'

'Because I'm only just born and have not got long to live and so would like to know as much as possible about the world,' it said all in one breath.

'Why bother?' said the elephant, who had just been woken up by the chattering butterfly.

'The information might come in useful,' it said.

'But it's too nice a day to go round asking silly questions,' yawned the elephant, and went to sleep again because the sun was so hot.

When the elephant woke it was almost dusk, and the flower was drooping, very bored. And sitting on its petals was the talkative butterfly. Still asking questions.

'How big is a tree?'
'How long is a river?'
'Why aren't moths beautiful?'
'Who lit the sun?'
'Why is grass green instead of pink?'
'Why is it growing dark?'

'Because it is the end of a lovely day.' The elephant answered the last question. Seeing that the flower was almost asleep, the butterfly flew on to the elephant's head.

'A lovely day? A lovely day? Why, I hardly noticed.'

'And now it is nearly night-time, so you've missed it,' said the elephant.

'So it is,' exclaimed the butterfly. And it flew away without even saying goodnight.

When the elephant and the flower woke up the next day, the butterfly had returned.

'Excuse me,' it said to the elephant, 'I forgot to ask you something yesterday, and it has been bothering me all night.'

'Really,' said the elephant. 'What is it?'

'I forgot to ask you what you meant by the phrase "a lovely day". I know all about—

monkeys and snakes and lions
and birds and flowers and rain
and tigers and elephants and
bushes and lilies and grass
and ponds and puddles and
rivers and other things but—

what is a lovely day?'

'Today is a lovely day,' said the elephant, 'like yesterday was.'

'O, is it really? Thank you,' said the butterfly.

And it began asking more questions. All day it asked questions. There were many other butterflies but it did not bother with them. It ignored everything that happened round it. It asked five hundred questions and when dusk came it flew off again, much to the relief of the elephant and the flower.

'That is the silliest butterfly I've ever seen,' said the elephant.

'Very silly indeed,' said the flower. 'It just asks questions and doesn't bother to enjoy itself.'

'Maybe it enjoys asking questions,' said the elephant.

'Maybe,' said the flower. 'But butterflies aren't born to go around asking questions.'

'I suppose not,' agreed the elephant. 'Do you think it will be back tomorrow?'

'I doubt it,' said the flower. 'Butterflies do not usually live for long.'

'A pity. The last few days have been quite lovely.' Then they both went to sleep.

That night huge clouds gathered over the trees, and the next day it rained and rained, and the butterfly did not come back.

The Man with the Sackful of Treasure

The elephant and the flower were sitting on the river bank listening to the river tell a story. It was the oldest story the river could remember, and it went like this:

'Once the jungle was in darkness and nothing knew what it was. The birds and the trees, the grasses and all the plants and animals were no more than black shadows. Flowers did not know they had colour and birds did not know they could sing. The trees did not know they grew fruit and the caterpillars did not know they became butterflies.

'Then into the darkness came a man with a large sack slung over his shoulder. "I'm a stranger here," he shouted, "and I seem to have got myself lost." And he promised he would give a piece of treasure from the sack to anything that could tell him where he was.

'Small voices began to whisper. All made suggestions as to where the man could be, but none really knew. They would have liked a piece of treasure, but decided it was best to be honest and admit that they did not know.

'Then one piece of the darkness, speaking for the rest, said, "I'm afraid we cannot help you. If we knew ourselves, we would be happy. In fact we would rather know where we are than have treasure."

'The man was delighted. "That's exactly the reply I wanted," he said. And from his sack he produced a red jewel and gave it to the darkness that had spoken first. The jewel became a rose, and in the black forest it glowed like a flame.

'Then something pushed its way through the darkness that was grass and came near to the man and the rose. It sat on a black rock and stared in amazement.

'The man noticed it. "If you were more than a lump of darkness, what would you like to do?" he asked.

'The thing near the rose said, "I would praise the rose with beautiful songs."

'Again the man was delighted. From his sack he took a bird. It was the whitest bird the jungle has ever known. There has been none to equal it since. And he gave the bird to the darkness and immediately it flew up on to his shoulder and began to sing. Next the man produced a tree in which the bird could live. It was a massive tree and each leaf was of a different shape and shade of green.

'The jungle grew slowly. From out of the darkness appeared more things,' said the river, 'and all amazed me. But I did not know what I was and became worried in case the man did not notice me and give me a gift from his sack. I waited blindly for him, seeing, on what later became my banks, the glowing birds and roses. They were like a frame round the darkness. Then the jungle began to whisper, "Something important is missing. There is something the tree and the bird and the rose all need."

'Hearing this I rushed on faster through the grass, making as much noise as possible in the hope that the man would notice me. And he did. He threw his sack down on to the grass and from it poured the water which I became.'

The elephant and the flower had listened very quietly to the river's story. It was a little complicated, they thought, but very strange and beautiful. The elephant was still curious.

'Did the man ever find out where he was?' he asked.

'Of course,' said the river. 'He found out that he was in the jungle.'

'And did anyone ever see the man?' asked the flower.

'Now that was a most peculiar thing,' sighed the river. 'Nobody ever did. But the more intelligent creatures have a theory that the man never really had a sack of treasure in the first place.'

'Then what did he give the darkness?' asked the puzzled flower.

'Bits of himself,' said the river.

How the Monkeys Came to Eat Bananas

Early one morning while it was still too dark to see anything, the King of the Monkeys sat in his tree eating a banana. This was long ago, before bananas were very common fruits for monkeys to eat. The King ate his banana secretly. He did not want the other monkeys to think him peculiar, like the lion who ate sunflowers.

Just as he finished his banana, the sun began to rise. The King of the Monkeys wondered about the sun. He wondered if it had anything to do with his banana. And so he ate another one. And, sure enough, the sun rose a little bit higher. He kept on eating bananas until the sun was well up in the sky and until he was too sick to eat any more.

The other monkeys gathered round the King's tree. He had been too involved in eating his fruit to notice them or hear them whispering about the banana-skins that lay at the bottom of the tree. Then the oldest monkey asked respectfully, 'Sir, why are you eating bananas?'

And the King said, King Monkeys always eat them. It's what makes the sun rise every morning. The other kings must have eaten them before me. I am the first king who has disclosed the secret.'

The monkeys stood round the King in silence. Indeed, it was a wonderful surprise. They had never thought monkeys had much purpose in the world. They all bowed respectfully to the King. 'Every evening before you go to sleep you must gather bananas for me,' he said. 'If I have to spend a long time gathering them, the sun might be late in rising.'

And so every evening before they went to sleep the monkeys ran round the jungle gathering bananas for the King. They did all this very quietly because, now that the King thought he made the sun rise, he went to sleep extra early in order to wake refreshed and ready for his bananas.

He soon grew fed up with eating bananas. In one week he ate over three hundred and became very sick. 'I can't do this any more,' he thought to himself. And so he called all the monkeys to a special meeting beneath his tree.

'I am going to delegate my great responsibility,' he told them. 'From now on you must all get up early and eat bananas. Just a few each, so the sun won't rise so far up that it disappears.'

The monkeys were very proud to be asked to share such a responsibility. They all bowed and hurried off into the jungle to collect bananas. From then on, the monkeys kept a few near them while they slept, and in the morning ate them eagerly, watching the sun rise as they did so.

They even began eating them in the afternoons, just to make sure the sun stayed up. And they thought that by eating green bananas they made it rain.

Truly, monkeys were very important!

They all smiled to see how easily they made the sun rise and rain fall. They never told the other jungle creatures of their secret, not even the flower, who loved the sun.

How the Kuputte-bird Brought Back the Sun for the Flower

Once, when it should have been dawn in the jungle, the sun did not come, and the jungle was left in darkness. The monkeys thought they had not eaten quite enough bananas, and so were not very worried. But the flower was worried. It asked the kuputte-bird to fly up into the stars and find out where the sun had gone.

'Certainly,' said the kuputte-bird, and it flew up into the sky until it was quite invisible.

'I hope the kuputte-bird can find the sun,' the flower said to the elephant. 'I'm very cold, and flowers can't live long without sunlight.'

'Don't worry,' said the elephant. 'It must be somewhere. Maybe it has overslept.'

'I doubt it,' said the flower.

Up and up and faster and faster flew the kuputte-bird. Soon it came to the moon.

'Have you seen the sun?' asked the bird. 'It seems to have got lost, and my friend the flower will die if I don't find it.'

'I saw it yesterday.' said the moon, 'and the day before that, and the day before that. In fact I've seen it every day since I've been here.'

'But have you seen it this morning?' asked the bird.

'This morning!' said the moon. 'This morning! You mean the day's come and everything's still dark? I thought I'd been here a long time!' And the moon grew very worried.

'You'd better go and ask the moon-owl who lives on the other side of me,' it said.

So the kuputte-bird flew round the moon until it reached the moon-owl.

'Have you seen the sun?' it asked.

The owl hadn't. 'You'd better ask the North Star,' it said. 'It knows most of what's going on in the universe.' And so the kuputte-bird flew up, faster and faster, for it knew that down on earth the flower must be growing very cold indeed.

Finally it reached the North Star.

'Have you seen the sun?' asked the bird. 'It seems to have got lost.'

'It is not lost,' said the North Star. 'It is alone sulking in a dark cave in the farthest corner of the universe.'

The kuputte-bird looked at the star in amazement. 'Why should it be sulking?' it asked.

And the North Star told it why.

'Once the sun was alone in the sky,' said the star. 'All the other stars and worlds were hardly born and were in darkness. The sun was bright and loved its own brightness. Nothing was so yellow, nothing was so red as itself. But as the centuries passed the sun grew tired of its own beauty, and it longed for something else to be as beautiful. The years passed, and mists and rains formed in the universe. The sun's beams travelled through these mists alone and it was sad that nothing else had appeared in the sky.
Then one day a rainbow was formed. Its colours were more numerous than the colours of the sun, and though it did not have the sun's power it had its beauty. The sun fell in love. It shone brighter and brighter because of its love for the rainbow. And its light and warmth reached many of the other planets, and as the sun grew brighter so did they. The universe woke and rejoiced in the sun's love.'

'Then why has it gone if it is so full of love?' asked the kuputte-bird, who thought the North Star's story very strange.

'Look around you,' said the star. 'Can you see a rainbow anywhere?'

The kuputte-bird looked. 'I can see only mist,' it said.

'Yes, and the mist has grown so thick and heavy that it has obscured the rainbow.'

'But the rainbow is still there, isn't it, hidden behind the mist?'

'Of course it's still there,' said the star. 'But the sun won't believe me and now it's gone away to pine.'

'Show me where it's gone to,' asked the kuputte-bird, 'and I'll try and bring it back again.'

So the North Star told the bird where to go. To the darkest cave in the farthest corner of the sky. And the kuputte-bird went there. It spoke to the sun but the sun would not listen. Even when it said the rainbow was only hidden, the sun still refused to come out of the cave. 'I don't believe you,' it said. 'I will only come out when I see the rainbow.'

So, round all the worlds and stars on which there was any form of life, the kuputte-bird flew, and wherever it landed it stopped for one moment to sing to the other birds, 'Come and help me, the sun is dying.'

And as it flew from each place, the birds that lived there followed. Soon the universe was full of beautiful, coloured birds. Led by the kuputte-bird they flew in the direction of the mists behind which the rainbow was hidden.

'Now,' said the kuppute-bird, 'beat your wings and sing. Form a wind such as the universe has not known before.' And the millions and the billions and the trillions of coloured birds beat their wings and sang. A great wind formed. The more they flapped their wings, the more the wind blew. It blew stronger and stronger until the mists began to move and fade.

Then from behind the mist the rainbow appeared again. It was the most beautiful rainbow the birds had ever seen. They sang its praise so loudly that the sun could not help but hear. 'I wonder what's happening,' it thought, and popped its head out of the cave to have a look. When it saw the rainbow again, it was so happy that it rushed back through the sky.

Down in the jungle the flower was writing its will. 'I leave everything I own to my friend the elephant,' it wrote.

And the elephant said, 'Thank you very much, but look, isn't that the sun coming out again, and don't you think it's getting rather warm?' And it was getting warm, very warm indeed – so warm that the flower ripped up its will and danced about on top of the hill.

'What happened to the sun?' asked the flower when the kupputte-bird arrived back on earth.

But the kuputte-bird was very tired and, yawning, said, 'I'll tell you tomorrow when I've had a good sleep.'

The Giraffe who Saw to the End of the World

Sometimes the giraffe came to the hill where the elephant and the flower lived. The giraffe had a very long neck, and when it stood on top of the hill and stretched its neck it could see over the trees and mountains to the end of the world.

One day the flower asked, 'What is the end of the world like?'

'Beautiful,' said the giraffe.

'What lives there?' asked the elephant.

'Giraffes, of course,' answered the giraffe.

The elephant had always thought elephants lived at the end of the world. And the flower had always thought only flowers could live in such a faraway place.

'Isn't there even *one* elephant there?' asked the elephant.

The giraffe stretched its neck as hard as it could. It looked across the trees and the mountains for a long time, and then said, 'No, only giraffes.'

'Maybe the giraffes are hiding a few flowers,' suggested the flower.

'Most certainly not,' said the giraffe.

'He's not telling the truth,' said a voice above them. It was the sparrow, who had been sitting all the time on the giraffe's head. 'I can see the end of the world a little better than he can, and it's full of sparrows. Very large sparrows, even larger than eagles.'

The giraffe said it had forgotten to mention sparrows, as they were smaller than giraffes. 'But there are definitely no elephants or flowers there,' it insisted.

'You're quite right,' agreed the sparrow.

The elephant and the flower decided to go for a walk instead of listening to the other two creatures, who were now boasting loudly. On their walk they asked all the creatures they met, 'What do you think lives at the end of the world?' And the ant-eater said ant-eaters, and the snake said snakes, and the pig said pigs and the lizard said lizards. And every single creature thought the only things that lived at the end of the world were just like themselves, only a little larger.

Later in the afternoon when the elephant and the flower returned to the hill, they found all the creatures they had met on their walk gathered round the giraffe. The giraffe and the sparrow had agreed that only giraffes and sparrows lived at the end of the world. They were telling the other creatures that there were lakes and forests and rivers and trees and even weeds there. But no other animals.

The animals were very indignant. 'We want to see for ourselves,' they shouted.

'You can't,' said the giraffe. 'You're not tall enough.'

'You can't,' said the sparrow. 'You've got no wings.'

Then the pig had one of its rare ideas. 'We'll all climb up the giraffe's neck and see for ourselves,' it said.

The giraffe didn't like the idea, especially as it was the pig's.

'It's a stupid idea,' it said. 'Fancy a pig trying to make a suggestion of any kind. It's bound to fail.'

But the other animals did not agree. They wanted to see the end of the world for themselves and they shouted and grunted so much that the giraffe had to agree to the pig's idea.

So first the snake climbed up. 'Just as I thought,' it said. 'The end of the world is full of snakes.'

'Nonsense,' squeaked the pig, and he began to climb up the giraffe, slipping every now and then. He clung to the giraffe's ears and shouted down: 'The snake's lying as usual. The end of the world's full of pigs. Very beautiful pigs. I can even see a King Pig sitting on a throne.'

'Rubbish,' shouted the ant-eater. 'Let's have a look.'

And when the ant-eater had reached the top it said, 'Why, what glorious ant-eaters there are! And so many ants to eat as well.'

'I still think that they're all wrong,' said the sparrow who was fluttering above the ant-eater. 'I'm the furthest up, and so have the clearest view. It's definitely sparrows.'

And so the creatures began to argue.

'High up is far enough up to see the end of the world,' they shouted at the sparrow. And the pig was so angry it nearly fell down.

'Take your feet out of my ears,' it squeaked at the ant-eater, who was sitting unsteadily on top of him. 'And take your hoof off my head,' shouted the snake.

As they argued, other creatures began to climb up the giraffe's neck. For miles and miles around, the jungle was full of talk and speculation about what lived at the end of the world.

Soon there was a gigantic pile of creatures on top of the giraffe's head. There were snakes and ant-eaters and pigs and frogs and monkeys and the white rabbit as well. Only the larger jungle creatures stayed on the ground with the elephant and the flower. They thought it a rather undignified heap, and knew quite well what lived at the end of the world.

The giraffe's neck was beginning to ache and strain.

All the time the creatures had been clambering over each other, a caterpillar had been slowly working its way up the giraffe's neck. It climbed on to the pig's head and stood upright. It was a very timid caterpillar and was a bit afraid of saying that the world was full of caterpillars. But it didn't have to anyway. The weight of all the creatures had become too much for the giraffe. It staggered on its feet, then tumbled down the hill. The creatures fell down on top of it in a huge heap. They all wriggled and groaned. And when they had untangled themselves they surrounded the caterpillar.

'It's your fault,' said the pig. 'It was your weight that made us fall. Now you'll have to settle the argument.'

The caterpillar was very afraid of the animals, and it didn't want to make them any angrier by saying the end of the world was full of caterpillars.

So it said: 'The end of the world's full of everything.'

Though the other creatures did not believe it, they were so relieved that it wasn't full of caterpillars they agreed that maybe the caterpillar could see best after all. And so they went home happy, leaving the flower and the elephant alone on the hill. It was getting dark anyway.

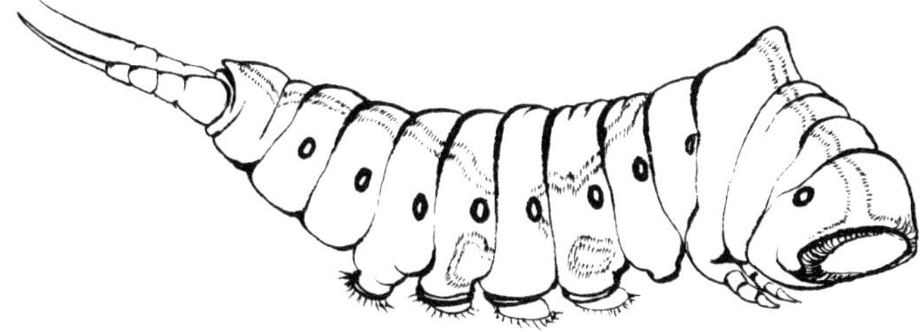

The Elephant's Petals

The elephant was sitting on the hill, looking at the clouds which all looked like very large elephants. Some days they looked like boats, and other days they looked like bushes, but today they looked best. He was very happy looking up until he noticed that the flower was acting rather peculiar.

It kept on walking round him, stopping every now and then and nodding its head, as if it were agreeing with itself about something.

'What's wrong?' asked the elephant.

'It has just occurred to me', said the flower, 'that you are a freak.'

'A freak!' cried the elephant. 'A *freak*!'

'Yes, a freak,' repeated the flower. 'You haven't got any petals. In fact you don't even possess an ordinary little leaf.'

The elephant had a small think.

'No, you're the freak,' he said. 'You haven't got a trunk.'

'Nonsense,' said the flower. 'I've seen plenty of things with petals and leaves – like blossoms and creepers and trees and bushes. Why, even the birds sometimes carry leaves – but they don't carry trunks. I've never seen anything with a trunk.'

'What about the trees, then?' said the elephant. 'What about *them*? They have trunks.'

'No, they don't,' said the flower. 'They have a very long and very thick stalk, like mine but a lot bigger. Anyway, it's not the same thing.'

'Yes, it is.'

'No, it isn't.'

'Yes, it is. They have leaves and trunks.'

'It isn't the same,' said the flower, getting angry.

'Of course it is,' said the elephant. 'You're just a small tree. More a small tree than I am a small elephant.'

'I'm not,' roared the flower. 'Trees have long wooden stems and you have a small, funny trunk. You're a freak! Try and name me something that has a trunk like yours.'

The elephant tried, but he couldn't. 'Then everything is a freak except me,' he shouted, and he ran down the hill as fast as he could. When he reached the bottom of the hill and was hidden in the jungle, he could still hear the flower shouting at the top of its voice, 'You're a freak! You've got no petals!'

And that was their first argument. The elephant grew very worried. Not about the argument but about the fact that he had no petals. 'Perhaps I should have some,' he thought. The flower had been very convincing.

Every time the elephant heard one of the jungle creatures coming towards him he scurried away behind a small bush or a large stone and kept very still. He was quite embarrassed about having no petals.

Then the elephant had an idea.
Farther upstream there was a native village.
'I'll go and see the witch-doctor,' thought the elephant.
But even the witch-doctor had no spells for growing petals on elephants, even very tiny ones.

'O well,' thought the elephant. 'I'll just have to go and find some old leaves myself and stick them on me.' And so he did.

The elephant walked round the jungle collecting fallen leaves and petals of all kinds. He made a huge pile of them, much bigger than himself. Then the elephant went and stood under a gum tree until he was all covered over in the messy stuff. Running back to the pile of petals and leaves he jumped into the middle of them, rolling over and over. They all stuck to the elephant.

All this time the flower had been sitting on the hill wondering what the elephant was doing.

'Maybe he's run away for ever,' thought the flower. And that made the flower very miserable. It decided to go and look for the elephant and apologize. After all, it was a silly argument. 'Elephants are elephants and flowers are flowers,' it decided to say when it found the elephant. It wandered down the hill and into the jungle, but it could not find the elephant.

At the edge of a path down which the flower was walking there was a strange little bump, entirely covered in petals and leaves.

'Funny,' thought the flower. 'I've never noticed that before.' It decided to sit on the bump and wait there just in case the elephant came past. But, before the flower could sit down, the bump gave a little groan and hurried away.

'That's a strange bump,' thought the flower. 'It's got little fat legs like an elephant. I'd better follow it.'

As the flower walked behind the bump, which did not seem able to see where it was going, it heard it say, 'I'm fed up. I'm very fed up indeed.' Then crash! – the bump banged into a large tree. It staggered about in circles, groaning all the time. The flower was deciding whether or not to ask the bump where it wanted to go and take it there, when they suddenly came to a shallow pond. Before the flower could shout a warning the bump, still dizzy, staggered in. Splash! went the pond. Groan! went the bump.

When the flower reached the pond it was full of petals and leaves, but there was no bump to be seen anywhere. In its place was the elephant, up to its neck in water.

'How peculiar,' thought the flower.

'I'm learning how to swim,' lied the elephant.

'That's good,' said the flower. 'I thought you might be drowning yourself because I said you're a freak.'

'Certainly not,' said the elephant. 'I don't like petals on me one bit.'

'That's good,' said the flower. And then it apologized and made a little speech it had prepared, about how elephants didn't need petals after all, and how flowers didn't need trunks either.

The elephant thought it was a marvellous speech and it got up out of the water and went home to look at the clouds again.

The Water-lily

At the source of the jungle river, miles from where the elephant and the flower lived, there grew a water-lily. It was anchored near the bank, sheltered from the sun by giant trees and cut off from the main flow of the young river by a makeshift island of water-grasses and old branches. On hot days, fish would shelter under its petals and tell it stories of their journeys up and down the river. They told it of the fierce eels and the gentle blue-fish; of the orange weeds and night stars that slept in eddies.

The lily loved to listen to the fish, and was happiest when they told it tales of other water-lilies – lilies equally as beautiful – that lived downstream.

As time passed it asked more and more questions about the other lilies. Although the fish were good company and the river cool and shaded by trees, it grew restless. One day it decided it must see the other flowers for itself. And so it persuaded the fish to chew through its stems so it could float along with the water. At first the fish said no, but so much did the lily plead that they finally gave in. 'You are not a fish,' they warned. 'You do not belong in the free-flowing water. You will grow old quickly once you have been set free.' But the lily did not care.

It floated downstream, sometimes tangling with the water-grass and sometimes with driftwood, but always it managed to keep moving. It began to learn many things about the river, but not enough to control the way it drifted. One morning after a rain-storm, when the river flowed particularly fast, it caught sight of another lily anchored to a stone at the water's edge. The lily was red, but bright and delicate. Round it hummed dragonflies and on its petals the shapes of clouds and trees were reflected. It filled with joy at the sight, and called for the red lily to join it. But the lily said, 'No, rootless I would grow old too quickly. My life is at the river's edge.'

So the lily floated on, though its sadness was mixed with happiness at seeing another lily. 'If I see nothing else,' it thought, 'it will not matter.'

Day and night the lily drifted downstream, and often it wanted to rest. Many of the fish it had known at the beginning of the river swam past underneath it. But they no longer spoke to the lily. Now it drifted freely, they could not rest beneath its petals. Still, the water-flower had other company now. Frogs would climb on to its large petals and drift lazily along, snapping up flies. But the company of water-snakes and frogs was not quite what the lily wanted.

Now after nine days and nights its memory of the red lily began to fade and it felt loneliness again. Yet it never felt sorry for itself or wished it was back at the beginning of the river. It had learnt more than most lilies, could speak with frogs and snakes, with the crocodiles and the kingfishers. It had seen many strange plants at the river's edge, had seen both the sun and the moon rise and set. Sometimes it even saw other lilies. Joyfully it shouted out to them, tried to catch on to a log or a drifting bush so it could slow down. 'Ask the fish to free you,' it called, but like the first lily they answered no. They did not wish to drift, and repeated what the fish had said: 'You do not belong in free-flowing water.'

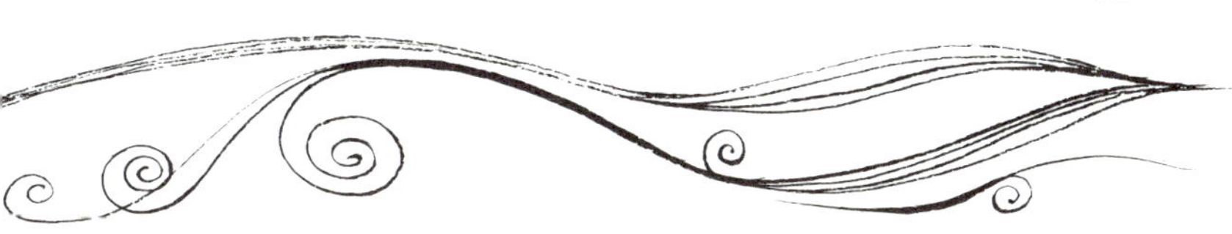

As the days went by the lilies became more numerous. In small groups, or alone in the shade, they sparkled. Beneath them the fish rested, and round them hummed the dragonflies. And none would follow the lily.

The river seemed never-ending. The lily grew old. On its fine petals blotches of yellow appeared. Water-flies bit into the petals, causing them to fray. Now the frogs could not sit safely on them, and the kingfishers, like the fish, ignored the lily. As its beauty vanished, so did the company of other creatures. It had grown to know the river well now. It could stop when it wanted at the bank's edge, though it only did so to rest at night. When in the day-time it saw the young lilies it no longer called out to them. Still, never did it long for or dream of the river's source where once it had lived. It remembered the shades

well, but had no wish to return there. Its life was the river's life: the reflections of stars, the singing of mysterious birds, the smooth, coloured stones beneath it. It loved the river, and each day its love was renewed with the sunrise. Yet it had grown weary now, and each time it rested it did so for longer periods.

'One day,' it thought, 'I will stop for ever.' And it did.

One night while the water-lily was sleeping, the river widened and split into many parts, each forming a small river of its own. The lily drifted into one of these rivers. It was a slow river, and led deep into the jungle, moving slower and slower as it went. The lily woke before dawn. It noticed the river's slowness and knew something had changed. And then it felt itself stop moving altogether.

As dawn broke and the river and jungle grew out of the darkness, so too grew the lily's happiness.

The old lily had arrived at a lake. Round it floated millions of other lilies. Mostly they were old, but together their colours made beautiful and intricate patterns on the surface of the lake. And each lily had a tale to tell about the river, about how they had begun their journey and what they had seen. And numerous creatures came down to the lake's edge to listen, and birds flew over them and fish slept beneath them. And the sun and the moon and the stars reflected on them multifold times, and the lily was glad it had not taken any advice when it was young. And the creatures called the lake the 'lake of ancient rainbows', and the old lily agreed with them all.

The Moonbeam-cutter

The elephant and the flower decided to go to the Forest of Moonbeams that grew up every night in a clearing in the jungle.

With the other creatures they often played on the edge of the forest. They never went deep into it, because then they would lose themselves.

The flower and the elephant played with their friend, the kuputte-bird. They played hide-and-seek in between the moonbeams and sometimes the kuputte-bird cheated and just stayed up in the air, too far up for the others to see him.

When it was tired the kuputte-bird said, 'I'm going home.'

'Let's stay a bit longer,' said the elephant.

'All right', said the flower.

They continued to play hide-and-seek together, and, each time one was found, the other hid deeper in the forest. And so soon they were both lost and couldn't find their way out again.

They wandered round and round among the moonbeams looking for ways out. But they just became more and more lost. Then they noticed that the Forest of Moonbeams was growing dimmer, bit by bit.

'I wonder what's happening?' said the elephant. 'The forest shouldn't fade out until daybreak.'

'I don't know what's happening,' said the flower, 'but I don't like it very much. Let's ask somebody the way out.'

Just then a mushroom said, 'Turn left at the third moonbeam on your right.'

'Is that the way out then?' they asked the mushroom.

'I'm not quite sure,' said the mushroom.

So they tried anyway. They turned left just as the mushroom had said, and in a clearing they found some small planets, sitting very quietly and looking worried.

'Shouldn't you be up in the sky,' asked the flower, 'marking the way for comets and spacemen?'

'We are waiting for the moonbeam-cutter,' said the small planets.

'The moonbeam-cutter?'

'He's a sort of wood-cutter,' said the planets. 'Only he cuts down moonbeams instead of trees. And he's so greedy he'll soon cut them all down.'

As they spoke, the elephant and the flower heard a distant crash. And the forest went a little dimmer.

'Soon we will all be moonbeamless and have nowhere to go in the day-time,' said the planets.

They explained that, though moonbeams were invisible in the day-time, they still existed, and the planets went invisible with them and had a good sleep.

Crash! The moonbeam-cutter had chopped down another beam. And again the forest grew dimmer.

It was a special forest.
The kind that should grow dim at dawn.
Invisible at dawn, not at night.

Crash! Dimmer and dimmer, and a bit dimmer. Crash!

'We can't think of any way of stopping him,' said the small planet in charge of the other small planets.

Then the elephant had one of his ideas. 'We'll all dream a nightmare,' he said.

'A nightmare?' said the planets. 'That would only frighten us.'

'Excuse my friend,' said the flower. 'You see, he's not very wise.'

'No, really,' said the elephant. 'We'll dream a nightmare.'

'We'd be too afraid,' repeated the planets.

'So would the moonbeam-cutter,' said the elephant. 'And because he is alone he will be more frightened.'

'Mmmmm,' said the small planets. 'Mmmmm. We see what you mean.' And so they agreed. And they called the other creatures who lived in the Forest of Moonbeams together.

And each dreamt a different part of the nightmare.
The birds dreamt a giant worm.
The owl dreamt a giant eye.
The elephant dreamt a five-headed mouse.
The flower dreamt a big greenfly with huge teeth.
And the planets dreamt a shuddering earthquake.

And so the nightmare looked awful. It had a long thin body and a giant eye and five heads with big teeth and wings, and it shuddered horribly when it moved. It was so horrible it became real.

It moved slimily through the Forest of Moonbeams. 'I'd like to eat a nice, fat moonbeam-cutter,' it thought.

The moonbeam-cutter was just about to chop down another beam when the nightmare saw him.

'Arrg!' screamed the moonbeam-cutter.

'Ah!' said the nightmare, 'my supper.'

It jumped on him and ate him, axe and all. Then, as it was not quite full and was very evil, it decided to come back and eat the flower and the elephant, and the birds and small plants and everything else it could get its teeth into.

But, before it reached them, they became so frightened they all woke up. But only just in time. The nightmare vanished just before it had decided what to eat with its five heads.

The elephant was very proud that its idea had worked so well, and the flower was a bit jealous, but thankful all the same.

'It's getting light,' said the flower.

'Is it?' said the elephant.

'Yes,' said the planets, 'it's nearly dawn.'

And it was. It seems the nightmare had taken a long time to dream up. Slowly the moonbeams and the planets and the birds and owls who lived in the forest faded as the sun crept up into the sky. And once again the elephant and the flower were in the jungle clearing. It was daylight, and they saw the hill on which they lived, green and lively by the river.

The Silver Ant's Dream

One day the elephant came to a place in the jungle where no birds sang and where nothing moved. It was a small glade in which stood one giant tree. No animals seemed to live there, and even the grass was still, and the wind did not blow at all. The elephant had never known such a quiet place.

In one of the twisting roots of the giant tree was a tiny door.

The elephant peered through the grass wondering what kind of creature could have built the door. He looked around until he noticed a grasshopper.

'Hello,' said the elephant, pushing its way through the grass. 'Did you build that door?'

The grasshopper did not answer. And when the elephant walked closer towards it, it disappeared. Next the elephant noticed a dragonfly, but the same thing happened. Silently, creatures kept appearing and disappearing. Sometimes there were as many as ten different animals and insects together in the glade, and other times the glade appeared quite empty.

Once the elephant saw either a giant dragonfly or a winged ant. He could not be certain, for either the ant had the most beautiful wings he had ever seen, or the dragonfly had an ant's body and legs.

'This is very disturbing,' thought the elephant. And he decided the door in the tree must have something to do with the mysterious glade. So the elephant opened the door and pushed his tiny body through. He found himself in a large wooden room and in the centre of the room, asleep on a leaf, was a huge silver ant. On either side of the ant stood a small ordinary ant. They stared at the elephant.

'Go away,' whispered the first ant.

'And quietly,' said the second.

But the elephant wouldn't. He was too curious. 'Do you live in this glade?' he asked.

'Of course not,' whispered the first ant.

'The glade does not exist,' said the second.

The elephant looked back through the door. The glade *seemed* to exist. There was the silent grasshopper, and up in the tree's branches was a peculiar bird. It had everything a bird should have, except that it also had antennae.

'I'm quite certain the glade exists,' said the elephant. 'I only walked through it a few seconds ago.'

'It does not matter how long ago you walked through it,' said one of the ants. 'It doesn't exist.'

'Not even when I can smell the grass?' asked the elephant.

'No,' said the ants.

The elephant stood inside the wooden room and became very confused. He wanted to shout at the ants. 'Maybe they are just mad,' he thought.

The ants explained that the glade was simply a dream of the silver ant, and now he had walked into the glade the elephant was also a part of the dream.

'You'd better go before the ant wakes up,' they said, 'or everything will disappear including yourself.'

'Pah!' said the elephant in disbelief. 'Don't be ridiculous.'

But he shouted too loudly, and the silver ant began to move. As it did so, the walls of the wooden room began to fade.

'Now see what you've done,' whispered the ordinary ants.

But the elephant did not stay around to see. He crashed out through the wafer-thin wood. 'Not only is everything ridiculous, it's also scary,' he yelled, as he fell down into the grass. Then the grass began to fade as well. In the tree there was a bird that suddenly lost its beak. And the grasshopper now floated about without any legs. The elephant had just climbed out of the glade when he heard the tree yawn. There was a popping sound and the whole glade disappeared. When the elephant turned round there was nothing to be seen but clusters of ordinary trees. He made sure he was still all there, especially his tail. Frightened, he went home and told the flower what had happened. But the flower just laughed.

That night the flower had a dream. It dreamt that there was another ant, much larger than the first, and this ant dreamt not only of a glade but also about eating flowers.

The flower didn't enjoy the dream one bit. And the next morning it even apologized to the elephant for laughing.

How the Sparrow Lost its Singing Voice

The worms were complaining about the sparrow again.

'We come up in the morning and gulp! – he eats us. We know it's the usual practice for sparrows, but this time he's gone too far.'

'Really?' asked the flower.

'How far?' asked the elephant.

'He's learnt our weakness for the theatre,' said the worms.

'For the theatre!' exclaimed the flower. 'I never knew worms liked the theatre.'

'Of course we do. And poetry. All worms have a weakness for it,' said the worms.

'I never knew that,' said the elephant.

And the worms explained how every morning the sparrow ran along the grass reciting 'I wandered lonely as a cloud', or some dramatic verse. 'It's irresistible,' said the worms. 'We come up spellbound to appreciate the verses and gulp! – we get eaten.'

'We were hoping you could stop him,' they said to the flower.

'I'll try,' it said. 'Come back later and I might have a plan.'

Soon after the worms had gone, the sparrow came along.

'Hello,' said the flower. 'I believe you've taken up an interest in the theatre.'

'The theatre?' said the sparrow. 'Who on earth told you that?'

'Some friends of ours,' said the flower.

'Do these friends have an irresistible desire for Shakespeare, by any chance?' asked the sparrow.

'As a matter of fact they do,' said the flower. And by the way, what's that you have hidden behind your back?'

'O nothing. Nothing at all,' said the sparrow.

'It's the complete works of William Shakespeare,' said the elephant, who had crept behind the sparrow to have a look.

'As a matter of fact it is,' said the sparrow. 'I wonder how it got behind my back like that.' And without waiting for the flower to say anything he flew away with the book between his claws.

When the worms came back the flower said, 'Why don't you form your own underground drama society, and then you won't have to come up and listen to the sparrow every morning?'

'That's a good idea,' said the worms. 'We will do that.' And so they did.

A few mornings later, before all the other birds had woken, the sparrow flew down on to the grass and started to recite. He recited a poem about daffodils seven times over and not a single worm came up to listen to him.

'That's funny,' said the sparrow, who was feeling peckish. 'I'd better try a bit of Shakespeare.

So he recited a few sonnets and something called a 'soliloquy', which isn't very easy for a sparrow at the best of times.

Still not a worm came up.

'I'd better go and look for berries instead,' thought the sparrow, whose belly had started to rumble and whose throat was very sore after so much reciting.

That night before going to sleep the flower and the elephant sat on their hill listening to the birds singing.

They saw the sparrow sulking in a bush. He was croaking rather badly.

'What's wrong with your voice?' they asked.

'I think I'm losing it,' said the sparrow.

'Is that all you've lost?' grinned the flower.

'No,' said the sparrow, 'I think I've lost my interest in dramatic recitals as well.'

The Side-stepping Pig

The dragonfly and the flower were sitting on a thorn bush talking to each other. They were having a very intelligent conversation about colours, and what was and what was not beautiful.

Then the pig came along.

'Hello, can I join you?' it asked.

'I don't think you would be very interested in our conversation,' said the dragonfly.

'Of course I would,' said the pig. 'Pigs are very good at conversations.'

'I'm afraid we're talking about things pigs don't understand very well,' said the dragonfly, wishing the pig would go away.

'Pigs understand everything,' said the pig.

'I doubt it,' said the dragonfly. 'We are talking about colours and beauty, and you must admit pigs aren't very colourful or beautiful.'

'And they don't have petals,' added the flower.

The pig's pride was hurt. It shook its head sadly. 'I'm afraid neither of you understand pigs very well.' And it sat down beneath the thorn bush. 'I'm going to stay here whether you like it or not,' it said.

The dragonfly and the flower continued to talk, ignoring the pig.

'My left wing reflects the sunset very nicely,' boasted the dragonfly.

'And I'm at my best in midsummer,' said the flower.

They were certainly very vain. They talked on and on about colour. About pink and blue and green and crimson and orange and yellow and mauve and brown and silver. The colours rolled poshly off their tongues and the pig listened.

It was very annoyed to be left out of the conversation. It tried hard to think of a colour or something beautiful that they had forgotten, but it couldn't. The only words that came to mind were pig-pen, mud, grease and slop. And the pig thought they wouldn't sound quite right, somehow. So the pig sulked away to the river.

It jumped up and down at the edge of the river, splashing itself clean. And then it rolled in some nice-smelling heather and finally polished itself on some special lavender leaves. Soon it became the most beautiful pig in the world. It sniffed itself twice, then returned to the river to look at its reflection.

When it was quite satisfied about its beauty the pig went home to its family. When they saw it the other pigs grunted and said, 'What an ugly pig. It's the most ugly pig in the world. Fancy a pig smelling like that.'

The pig was hurt. It wanted very much to be a beautiful pig and have good conversations, but somehow everything seemed to be going wrong today.

As it wasn't much wanted anywhere, the pig went off into the jungle and brooded about beauty and ugliness, and pig-pens and colours. Then it had an idea that made it

very excited. It went back to the pig-pen and lay on its side in the mud until it was quite filthy on one side but still clean on the other. Then it practised walking sideways and talking out of the corner of its mouth.

In this way the pig managed to spend the rest of the day side-stepping between the pig-pen and the thorn bush. As there was no wind now, the pigs did not smell the lavender-scented side of the pig, and the dragonfly did not smell the pig-pen side of the pig.

The pig was very happy with the arrangement, but still confused. It was the only side-stepping pig in the world. It wished with all its heart that everyone had the same ideas about what was beautiful; then it would not have to side-step.

'It would save a lot of bother,' thought the pig.

The Elephant and the Ghost

It was midnight in the jungle.

The flower was asleep, dreaming of bees and butterflies.

Suddenly it was woken by a little scream.

It was the elephant.

'What's wrong?' yawned the flower.

'I'm scared,' said the elephant, and screamed a bit more.

'What on earth is there to be scared of?' asked the flower.

'That,' said the elephant, and pointed down into the trees at the bottom of the hill.

Down in the jungle, jumping about in the thick mist, was a strange white shape. It jumped over the dark outlines of the bushes and then disappeared behind the trees.

'Let's go and find out what it is,' said the flower, trying to be brave.

'You go alone,' said the elephant. 'Elephants don't like ghosts very much.'

'A ghost!' said the flower. 'A ghost! Why didn't you tell me it was a ghost? Flowers like ghosts even less than elephants do.'

The flower had stopped yawning and was very much awake. The thought of going into the jungle alone made its petals curl up. 'You're a coward,' it said to the elephant.

'I admit it,' replied the elephant. 'Specially where ghosts are concerned.'

They sat on the hill as quietly as possible. The strange white shape had begun to move about again. 'Do you think it's seen us?' whispered the elephant.

'Shussssh!' shushed the flower. 'Shussssh!'

After a long time the thing moved deeper into the trees and disappeared from sight. It took the elephant and the flower a long time to go back to sleep and when they did they both had nightmares.

The next morning they decided it was safe to go into the jungle because it was light now. They went in among the trees where they had seen the ghost, but there was nothing there. 'Maybe we both had the same nightmare and never really woke up,' said the elephant hopefully. 'Maybe it was a bit of the nightmare we dreamt in the Forest of Moonbeams.'

The flower didn't like that idea one bit. 'Of course it wasn't,' it said. 'We would need all the moonbeam creatures to help us make *that* nightmare again. And they wouldn't.'

'Well, let's ask the kuputte-bird if he saw the ghost,' suggested the elephant. 'If he saw one then it must have been a real ghost.'

'That's a good idea,' said the flower.

And they asked the kuputte-bird.

'Yes I did see it,' the bird said.

'A pity,' they said.

And all morning the three of them sat at the bottom of the hill and wondered what to do about the ghost.

They decided they would be brave and watch a bit closer.

So that night instead of going to sleep they all hid in a bush and waited for the ghost to come. But it was very misty and they could not see far out of the bush. They sat very quiet and waited for something to happen.

Then something did happen.

Something sprang up in the grass quite near them. It came so suddenly they forgot they were supposed to be watching it and rushed up the hill screaming.

'We are not very brave, are we?' said the elephant.

'No,' said the flower.

'I agree,' said the kuputte-bird.

On the third night the kuputte-bird and the flower made up a plan that the elephant did not like one bit.

'We'll dress you up to look like a ghost and maybe you will scare the real ghost away,' they said.

'Why me?' asked the elephant.

'Because you're the bravest,' lied the bird and the flower.

And because the elephant liked the idea of being the bravest, he said, 'All right.' When he realized what had been said he was very annoyed with himself.

They put a white sheet over the elephant and made him practise moaning and groaning. Then they all hid in the bush again, as it was near midnight.

'It's only a small ghost after all,' comforted the flower.

'And I make an even smaller one,' moaned the elephant.

'Now when the ghost comes we are going to push you out of the bush very fast so you'll surprise it.'

The elephant was so frightened he didn't protest.

At midnight the ghost appeared again.
It hopped up and down.
Backways and sideways.
'One, two,' it said. 'One, two, three, hup!'

The elephant thought the ghost must be a very mad ghost, but before he could change his mind about the plan, the flower pushed him out of the bush.

He went crashing through the twigs, all tangled in the sheet, and rolled to a stop in front of the little white thing.

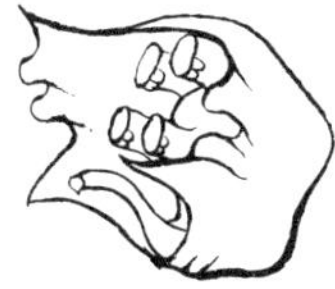

'*Arrrrg*!' screamed the little white thing, and fainted with fright.

'That's funny,' thought the flower who was still hiding in the bushes. 'I never thought ghosts would be quite so scared of other ghosts.'

'What does the ghost look like?' whispered the kuputte-bird who was in the bush with the flower. They were afraid it might wake up at any moment.

But the elephant did not answer. He just laughed under his sheet. 'O dear! He-he-he-heee-he-he-he-he-ha!' He laughed and fell about in the dark grass and he couldn't stop giggling.

The other two thought he had gone mad.

'Come out and have a look for yourselves,' said the elephant when he had stopped laughing.

The flower and the kuputte-bird slowly crept from the bush and edged their way towards the elephant and the ghost. When they were quite near, the ghost sat up and rubbed its eyes.

'Fancy that!' laughed the flower, when it saw what was sitting on the grass.

It was the white rabbit who had been doing his nightly exercises.

'I don't think it's very funny,' grumbled the rabbit.

And it hopped away without ever knowing what a scare it caused in the jungle.

The Wise Mule

'Is this a magic jungle?' the elephant asked the flower.

'I don't know,' said the flower. 'It's the only jungle I've ever lived in.'

'Is this a magic jungle?' the elephant asked the kuputte-bird. 'I don't know,' replied the strange bird, 'but I've never seen another kuputte-bird.'

'Is this a magic jungle?' the elephant asked the Forest of Moonbeams.

'We couldn't tell you,' they replied. 'We've slept nowhere else.'

And the elephant asked many creatures if the jungle was a magic jungle. And none of them really knew. Not the monkeys who made the sun rise, nor the giraffe who saw to the end of the world.

So the elephant sat under a cactus tree that grew near the swamp-land, and it fell asleep. When it woke again it knew that the jungle must be magic, for it had had a dream in which it asked a mule the same question.

'Of course it is,' the mule had replied. 'If you lived in an ordinary jungle you would never ask such questions! In ordinary jungles elephants don't dream of mules, and mules don't answer questions.'

And then the mule had vanished.

How the Elephant Became Very Big

Once there was a creature that dived through a raindrop and was never seen again. Except very briefly by the flower.

The creature was called the Plinkinplonk, and it was a friend of the elephant and the flower. When it disappeared they decided to go and look for it, with rather disastrous consequences.

The flower and the elephant were sitting on the hill. 'The Plinkinplonk has been gone a long time,' said the elephant.

'I'm afraid it's got lost,' said the flower.

'Maybe it is just sleeping somewhere,' replied the elephant.

'I doubt it,' said the flower. 'Plinkinplonks never sleep. They dream, but never sleep.'

'Then it must be dreaming somewhere,' suggested the elephant.

'It might be,' said the flower, 'but we had better go and make quite sure it's not lost.'

So they went down the hill, which though they didn't know it was for the very last time, and they looked for their friend in the jungle.

'Has the Plinkinplonk come this way?' they asked the path.

'No,' said the path.

'It came across me,' said the grass.

So the elephant and flower went across the grass in search of their friend the Plinkinplonk.

It was the very last Plinkinplonk in the world. Even rarer than pandas. And when it died, Plinkinplonks would become extinct. It was a very unusual creature. Impossible to describe because it kept on changing shape and size according to its moods. It was the only creature that ever left its dreams floating about in the grass, like bubbles. And sometimes they took days to fade away.

After they had been looking a long time they found a bit of the Plinkinplonk's latest dream. It was floating in a small bubble and was only a little faded.

'It must have passed this way quite recently,' said the flower.

'What on earth's inside this?' asked the elephant, poking its trunk at the bubble.

'A large raindrop and a tree,' said the flower. The flower recognized the tree. It was a large, twisted oak that the Plinkinplonk often sat beneath.

They arrived at the tree just in time to see the Plinkinplonk dive from the topmost branch.

Splash! It dived deep into the raindrop.

'It must have made itself very small to do that,' said the elephant.

'It's rather a large raindrop,' replied the flower. And so it was. Even larger than the head of a sunflower.

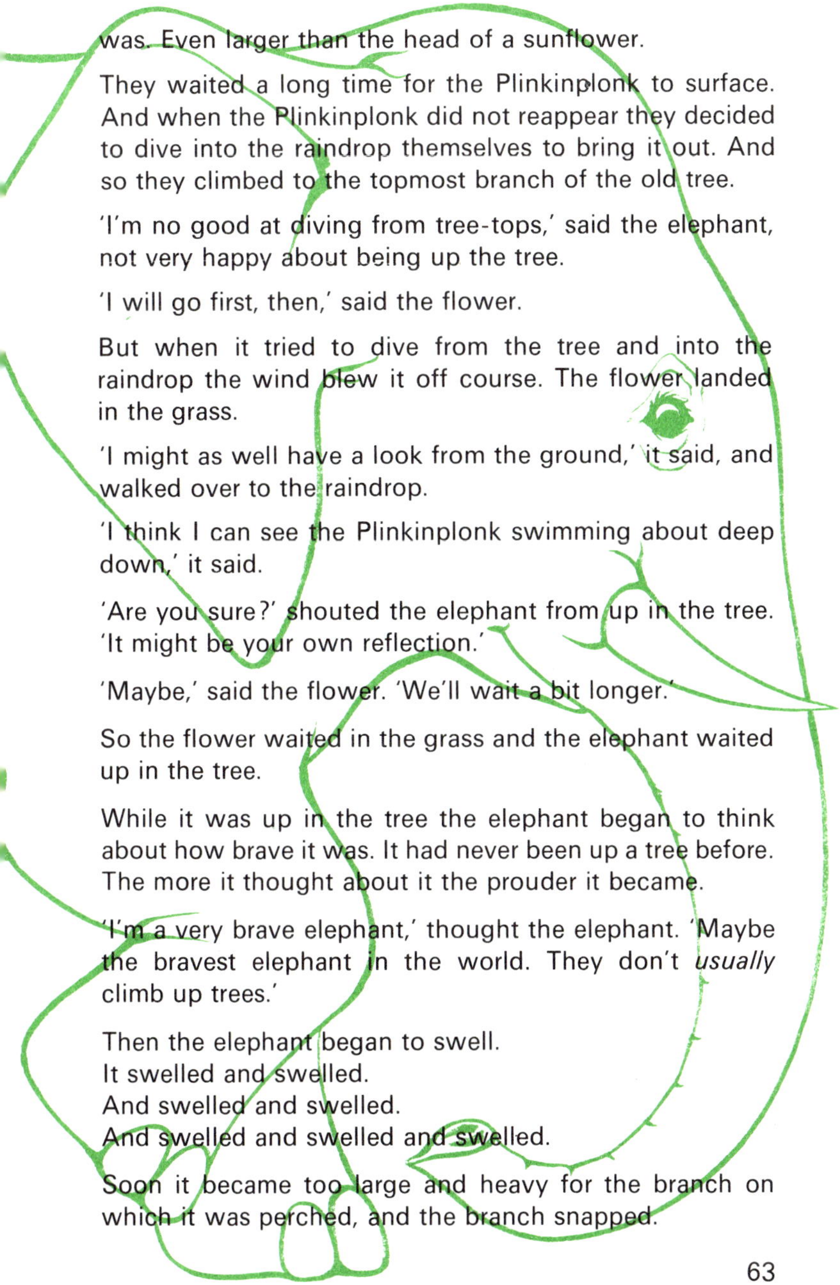

They waited a long time for the Plinkinplonk to surface. And when the Plinkinplonk did not reappear they decided to dive into the raindrop themselves to bring it out. And so they climbed to the topmost branch of the old tree.

'I'm no good at diving from tree-tops,' said the elephant, not very happy about being up the tree.

'I will go first, then,' said the flower.

But when it tried to dive from the tree and into the raindrop the wind blew it off course. The flower landed in the grass.

'I might as well have a look from the ground,' it said, and walked over to the raindrop.

'I think I can see the Plinkinplonk swimming about deep down,' it said.

'Are you sure?' shouted the elephant from up in the tree. 'It might be your own reflection.'

'Maybe,' said the flower. 'We'll wait a bit longer.'

So the flower waited in the grass and the elephant waited up in the tree.

While it was up in the tree the elephant began to think about how brave it was. It had never been up a tree before. The more it thought about it the prouder it became.

'I'm a very brave elephant,' thought the elephant. 'Maybe the bravest elephant in the world. They don't *usually* climb up trees.'

Then the elephant began to swell.
It swelled and swelled.
And swelled and swelled.
And swelled and swelled and swelled.

Soon it became too large and heavy for the branch on which it was perched, and the branch snapped.

The elephant came crashing down from the tree, crushing both the raindrop and the Plinkinplonk inside it.

'O dear,' thought the elephant when it realized what had happened. It had eliminated Plinkinplonks for ever.

The worse thing was it had grown very big and everything else had grown very small.

'Where are you?' it shouted to the flower.

'I'm here!' squeaked a tiny voice.

When the elephant looked down it saw a small blue speck in the grass. 'I can hardly see you from here,' it said. 'Your voice is hardly a whisper. In fact I'm not sure if it's your voice or the wind.'

They grew miserable. Now they could no longer play together or live together on the hill.

'I shouldn't have been so big-headed,' moaned the elephant. 'Then I might not have swollen.'

The flower tried to sound happy. 'Maybe you were meant to be that big,' it said.

'Maybe,' agreed the elephant.

The sun was setting. They sat together talking about how good things had been when they were the same size. And then the flower said, 'It's time for me to go back and sleep.'

The elephant also wanted to return to the hill, but now it was much too large. 'I'll go and look deeper into the jungle,' it said.

'All right,' said the flower and it turned away into the long grass and soon disappeared.

The elephant stood beneath the trees thinking how different the jungle suddenly looked. It hesitated in leaving, and then shouting goodbye it lumbered away in the opposite direction.